WATCH OUT!

At Home

Honor Head

WAYLAND

Explore the world with **Popcorn** - your complete first non-fiction library.

Look out for more titles in the **Popcorn** range. All books have the same format of simple text and striking images. Text is carefully matched to the pictures to help readers to identify and understand key vocabulary.
www.waylandbooks.co.uk/popcorn

First published in 2009 by Wayland

Copyright © Wayland 2009

Wayland
338 Euston Road
London NW1 3BH

Wayland Australia
Level 17/207 Kent Street
Sydney NSW 2000

Editor: Jean Coppendale
Designer: Alix Wood
Picture research: Taglines Creative Limited

British Library Cataloguing in Publication Data:
Head, Honor
    At home. - (Popcorn. Watch out!)
    1. Home accidents - Prevention - Juvenile literature
    I. Title II. Series III. At home
    363.1'37-dc22

ISBN 978 0 7502 5793 0

Printed and bound in China

Wayland is a division of Hachette Children's Books,
an Hachette UK Company.
www.hachette.co.uk

Photographs:
Cover iofoto/Shutterstock; 4 Baloncici/
Shutterstock; 5 Marilyn Barbone/ Shutterstock;
6 Fancy/Veer/Corbis; 7 Vasiliy Koval/
Shutterstock; 8 moodboard/Corbis;
9 Solus-Veer/ Corbis; 10 iofoto/Shutterstock;
11 Kelpfish/Shutterstock; 12 pixland/ Corbis;
13 Monkey Business Images/ Shutterstock;
14 Corbis; 15 Fancy/ Veer/Corbis;
16 Shutterstock; 17 Roger Ressmeyer/Corbis;
18 Fancy/ Veer/ Corbis; 19 Juan Jose Lopez/
Shutterstock; 20 Thomas M Perkins/
Shutterstock; 21 Kiselev Andrey Valerevich/
Shutterstock.

🏠 Contents

What is dangerous at home?

Your home is a safe place but you can still have accidents there. Watch out for dangerous things around the house.

In the kitchen the oven, cooker tops and pans can be hot.

If you have a garage or garden shed, watch out! There may be sharp tools inside that can give you a nasty cut.

All these garden tools could be dangerous. Some are sharp and some are heavy.

 # Furniture

Climbing on furniture is dangerous – you could fall. If you have to stand on a chair to reach something, make sure the chair is steady.

If possible, ask an adult to get something for you if it is high up.

Shut doors and push drawers closed from the front. You can trap your fingers when you close cupboard doors and drawers.

Keep fingers away from cupboard and fridge doors when you close them.

🏠 Tidy up

Always put toys away when you have finished playing with them. If you leave them lying around, you or someone else might trip over them.

Have fun playing but always tidy your things away afterwards.

Never leave anything such as toys,
books or clothes on the stairs.
Someone might not see them
and have a nasty fall.

Leaving toys
on the stairs
could cause
an accident.

🏠 In the kitchen

Cooking is fun, but you need to be careful in the kitchen. Saucepans and cookers can get very hot.

When ovens are on they are hot and can burn you.

When water boils it makes steam. Steam from a saucepan or kettle can hurt you.

Watch out for pot and pan handles. Be careful not to knock them over.

steam

Keep your arms and hands away from steam.

🏠 Cooking and eating

Take care with sharp objects such as needles, nails, pins and knives. Always ask an adult to help you with a sharp knife.

Ask an adult to help you cut, or peel, fruit and vegetables.

It is best to stand still or sit at a table when you eat and drink. Walk carefully if you are carrying anything made of glass.

Try to sit down to eat and drink.

Blow on your food to make sure it's not too hot before you take a bite.

 # Fire

Fires keep us warm and cosy when it is cold but they can burn. It is dangerous to play too close to a fire.

There should always be a fireguard in front of a burning fire.

Only adults should use matches
or fire lighters. Always make sure
that candles are blown out
properly after they are used.

Wax from a candle
is hot and even a
drip can burn you.

15

It's electric!

We use electricity every day to make things work. Electricity comes into your home through a socket and plug in the wall.

Only put electric plugs into sockets.

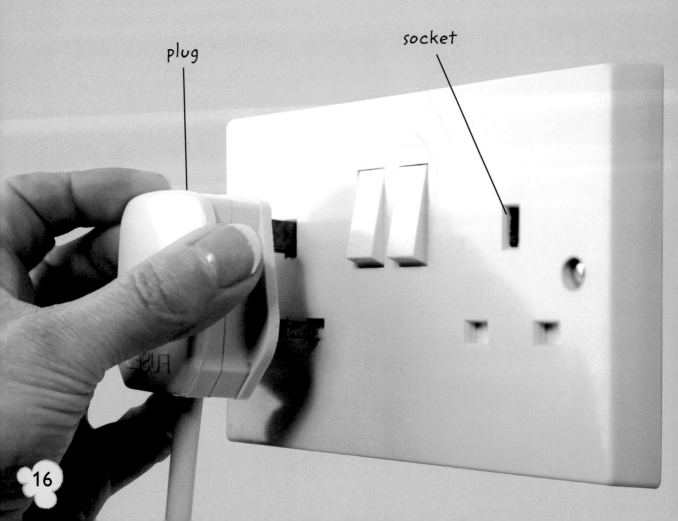

plug

socket

You should never use anything electrical in the bathroom. Water and electricity are very dangerous together because they can give you a bad shock.

Never touch anything electrical with wet hands.

Dry your hair in the bedroom.

 # Water

Before you wash your hands or have a bath or shower, test the water to make sure it is not too hot.

What would happen if the tap water is too hot?

Puddles of water on a bathroom
floor can make it very slippery.
Use a bath mat to make sure you
don't slip on a wet floor.

bath mat

Do not touch

Lots of bottles are filled with liquid that can make you very sick. Only touch bottles when you know what is in them. Ask an adult if you're not sure.

These bottles are filled with cleaning liquid that can be dangerous.

Some tablets can look a lot like sweets but if you eat them they will make you ill. Only eat a sweet if you know exactly what it is.

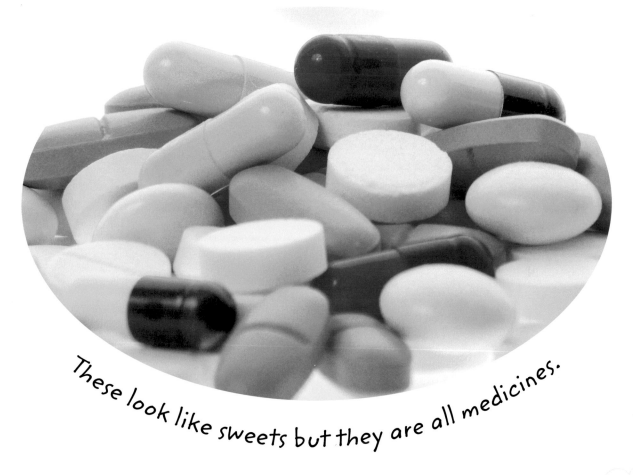

These look like sweets but they are all medicines.

What's safe and what's not?

Match a sentence with a picture to see what is safe and what isn't, at home. Answers on page 24.

1. Some medicines can look like sweets.

2. Watch out that the water is not too hot.

3. Steam can burn – be careful.

4. Play time is fun but put your toys away in a safe place.

5. Never touch electrical things, such as a hairdryer, with wet hands.

6. Enjoy cooking but be careful near hot ovens.

Glossary

electricity   this is a form of power that you use to make things work. You use electricity for lights, computers and televisions.

fire lighters   something used to light candles or fires

medicine   tablets or liquids that you take when you are not well

plug   this goes on the end of wire and is put into a socket on the wall. A socket and plug give you electricity.

steady   when something doesn't move or wobble

tools   things you use to help you to do something. In the garden you use tools, such as a spade, to help you dig.

Index

Answers to puzzle: 1e, 2d, 3f, 4b, 5c, 6a